DADDY,

IF YOU ONLY KNEW...

The Voices of the Children

Steve & Lennette Deal

5 Fold Media

Visit us at www.5foldmedia.com

(handwritten inscription) Blessings Nate! Thank-you for the blessing you are. Heb 10:35,36

Pastors Steve & Lennette Deal 7/30/10

We pass through many seasons in our lives as we grow and mature. Along the way, there are people who impact us positively and negatively, and there are many situations and circumstances that change us as well. All my life I have heard the phrase "iron sharpens iron." I keep thinking that my iron must be pretty sharp by now, especially since we first entered the ministry twenty-three years ago. One thing that remains constant is the Word of God, which says, "And we know that God causes everything to work together for the good of those who love God and are called according to His purpose for them" Romans 8:28. I am so glad that no matter how bad a situation may look, God always works it out for the good because I am His child. You too can have that same reality.

God birthed this book in our hearts four years ago, as we ministered in a community that was once voted the fifth worst place in the nation to raise kids. It was a place people often avoided, but we saw the beauty. This city became our favorite place to be. God rooted our hearts in that community. He gave us a burden and a love for the amazing people who battled life there every day. God called me to work with the children and youth of that town, and as I invested in their lives, some deeper than others, I began to see the impact of a great missing link... a daddy. I started hearing their voices. **This book is dedicated to all the children around the world who need to be heard in regards to this missing piece in their lives, their daddy.**

I also dedicate this book to my parents, Art and Shirley Cheek, who have been the greatest examples of godly parents I could have ever dreamed of or asked God for. I have included a letter to my Dad toward the end of this book because I want him to know how much he has truly impacted my life and the life of my family on a daily basis. This impact comes from the fact that not a day goes by that he cannot be found praying for the world and his family. His prayers have interrupted the heavenlies on our behalf. I have also included his letter to give others hope that today can be the first day of a new life for them and their children. It is not too late for this to become your heritage. I wish that all of the precious children that I had the privilege to work with in a pocket community of Tampa, Florida, could have had the gift that I had in my parents. For this reason and a thousand more, Mom and Dad, I dedicate this book to you.

All our love, Lennette and Steve

ACKNOWLEDGEMENTS

First and foremost, we are extremely grateful to the Lord of our experience, Jesus Christ.

To my lovely wife, it is from your passion for the downtrodden and the orphan that this book was birthed.

To our children, Brianna and Jordan, we were always petrified at the thought of parenting, afraid we would mess up. In spite of us, you guys turned out to be amazing people, having hearts for God and loving the people made in His image. Ruthy, as our new daughter-in-law, we count you as a gift to this family! Your youthful spirit keeps us all young.

To Mom and Dad Cheek, words cannot express the appreciation I have for ALL you have done for us since we said yes to the Lord and His calling on our lives.

To Mom and Bob, you were "both" the Dad I never had. Thanks for your support, encouragement, and love.

To my brothers Dan and Rich, who walked out the story of our Dad with me.

To our extended family and friends, your deposits in our lives have made it possible for us to write this book.

To Mer, for being my wife's best friend for over 40 years.

To Papa Mike and Momma Elaine, Pastors of White Dove Fellowship, New Orleans, Louisiana, your wisdom and spiritual parenting have been invaluable. We see things differently in the Kingdom because of you.

To Rev. Cal and Sandy Garcia, your friendship and mentoring have made a forever imprint on our lives.

To Mike and Christina Kelley, no spiritual Papa could be more proud of a son and daughter.

To Elmer Nugent, for your wisdom, character, and encouragement at just the right time.

To Rev. Wayne and Pat Tiggett, for being faithful friends.

To Kesha, De, Quan, Kel, Kish, Faith, and Chris, you've brought us such joy, and other "joys" as spiritual parents. Keep reaching up and not down.

To All Nations Outreach Center, for the privilege of being your pastor for over 10 years. Many lives were touched with the Gospel because of you.

To Michael Nelson, a beautiful soul and wonderful father. One of the greatest pastors I know. My hero and friend. I want to be like Mike.

To Malcolm Burleigh and Zollie Smith, and my brothers on the NBF, thank you for making history in the AG. Press on in the struggle.

To Dr. Suuqiina and Quamaniq, for helping us to understand the Creator in a way that brings Him honor.

To my co-laborers in the faith, the many ministers that we have forged a relationship with over the years. We need each other.

To all of our new friends at Morningstar in Fort Mill, South Carolina, what a rich spiritual environment and a proverbial breeding ground for creativity and fellowship.

To our spiritual kids, friends, and those in whose lives we had a part in Holland, Michigan.

TABLE OF CONTENTS

I. THE VOICES OF THE CHILDREN

II. LET THE HEALING BEGIN

III. HOPE IN ACTION

I am blessed and privileged to write the foreword to a book that represents the heart of children and the healing that God provides through their honesty.

I have spent over thirty years as an educator and football coach pouring into the lives of young men. After reading in the local newspaper that one of my past students had committed a very serious crime, I realized that while I taught him how to play the game of football, I did not teach him how to live.

Today, Abe Brown Ministries, through its diverse programs such as its Transitional Living Program, is dedicated to returning men to their proper place in faith, family, and community.

Pastor Steve and Lennette Deal's work with children and young people in urban Tampa has had a powerful impact and has been an effective tool to prevent these children from becoming statistics in the criminal justice system.

Daddy, If You Only Knew

As you read, you will experience the Holy Spirit's transforming and healing power in your own life. From the pens of these children, you will experience their pain, and the longing to be loved, nurtured, and taught by their Father.

Abraham R. Brown
Abe Brown Ministries
Founder & CEO

The enemy does not have to do anything secretive, sly, or even sneaky to destroy America. He is doing it from within by removing the fathers from the home, causing them to forget their place as the spiritual head of the home. Through this deep hurt, the cycle repeats itself over and over again through their children, if those children do not find personal healing.

At the same time, there are men who have been examples and taken their rightful place as the head of the household and who have loved their children with their whole heart. This book houses their voices as well.

The Word says in Ephesians 6:1-3, "Children, obey your parents in the Lord, for this is right. 'Honor your father and mother.' This is the first commandment with a promise- 'that it may go well with you and that you may enjoy long life on the earth.' "

But how do you honor someone who has abused and neglected you? God does not qualify Ephesians 6:1-3 based on circumstances. "Honor" does not mean condone or approve. It means to show respect. God can help each one of us find a way to honor those fathers who have hurt us. You will see at the back of this book how God helped my husband to honor his father, despite the pain his father caused. This is not an easy task, but you are not alone.

I believe God is calling our nation to begin to honor the fathers of our faith as well as those who have laid the groundwork of our lives. Namely, the freedom of our faith, revivalists, prophetic movements, and the foundational principles which were based on the truth of His Word. As we begin to apply this very powerful truth of His Word in our homes, honoring our fathers and our forefathers, we will see the bleeding stop and our homes and nation healed.

We have got to pray and take action. That may mean being uncomfortable or subjecting yourself to the possibility of rejection, but the outcome will be healing. You are not responsible for how someone responds to what you do according to His Word; you

4

are only responsible for being obedient to the Word. Obedience is always the key to a free life.

"If my people, who are called by my name, will humble themselves and pray and seek my face and turn from their wicked ways, then will I hear from heaven and will forgive their sin and will heal their land." II Chronicles 7:14

I.
The Voices of
the Children
Lennette Deal

Daddy, if you only knew…

This is for all you fathers who aren't there and have no idea how your children feel because you're always missing the dance recitals, football games, soccer games, and band rehearsals. This is for fathers who need to step up and put the work aside and be there for your children and stop worrying so much about you. The main cause for divorce is when the fathers are constantly absent; you are either at your job making money or out drinking or cheating on your wives. (You know who you are.)

STEPPING UP
Fathers, it is time for you to step into your children's lives. If you only knew how much we missed you, you would make yourselves step up, take the

positions God has placed you in, and stop making your wives work and do everything in the house. You need to take out the trash, mow the lawn, and clean the garage. These days, men complain about how tired they are when they come home, yet most women work more than you do. The message here is STEP UP!

DADDY, IF YOU ONLY KNEW

Here are some letters written by children and teens about what they feel. As you read the letters, realize that they are real and that there is a purpose for you to read this book. These letters show not only how children feel when you are not there, but also how much they love you. We hope to make you feel good through their words.

**5 Fold Media has intentionally allowed some misspelled words, grammatical errors, and unique fonts and sizes throughout the book in order to allow the variety of a child's touch to be displayed.

Chapter 1

Voices

VOICES

Imagine a young man who is handsome, athletic, and musically talented, with great dreams, but whose face always appears angry and hard because at the very core of those dreams is one desire, one longing to have a dad in his life who really cares, someone who will greet him at the locker room after a football game and say "Great job, son" or maybe make it to practice and give him some pointers. This young man would even have welcomed a loving rebuke just to have a dad around to give one, but he didn't have one. So he took that rage and that anger and funneled it into hits on the football field and two drum sticks meeting the heads of a drum set on a church platform. But right now, if you were to talk to this amazing young man, he would tell you he would trade all of his accomplishments for a dad who loves him and cares about his present situation and his future. This is a real young man, trying to press through daily life as a teenager without a father's direction. What about this young man's voice?

She is a beautiful young lady, a rising star, about to ride in her first Corvette around the football field. It is the homecoming game and her day to shine. She has risen above all her obstacles; there have been a lot of them, but she perseveres. Affording the dress for such an occasion was an obstacle, but through a financial miracle, she looks like a princess. Any dad would be proud to call her his, but he isn't there. He doesn't see her waving her hands to the crowd. He doesn't see her beautiful smile as she watches one of her dreams come true. He could have. You see he chose not to come. The only thing standing in his way was a decision to go or not to go. No job stopped him. No crisis stopped him. He was home doing absolutely nothing of significance. This was his opportunity to watch his baby girl's dreams come true. This young lady is real. What about her voice?

She is around nine years old and is oh, so angry. She is about forty-five pounds of trouble, wiry and feisty. She can start a fight in any venue; just give her one small reason to disagree with you, one moment of correction, make just one attempt to tame her, and you have an imaginary fighting ring with fists flying, legs kicking, and words coming out of her mouth that are rated R. Would you be angry if you had no idea who your daddy was? What if you came home from school sometimes to be locked out of the house and stuck on a porch in ninety degree weather for hours and no daddy to rescue you like you see in the movies or in children's books? You would be waiting for someone to come home and unlock the door so you weren't subject to the three hundred child predators in your zip code.

Get this little girl calm long enough and you can hear her dreams. They have to do with her dad, a dad she does not know but longs to play with and get to know. She has dreams of trips to Busch Gardens and Disney World. If this little heart is not healed, she may wind up in our jail system with all her anger and bitterness. Now there is still a soft spot, wanting to play. Someone needs to save her. What about this little girl's voice? Should it be heard?

What about a little twelve-year-old boy, being raised by a great-grandmother because mom, dad, and grandmother are all in jail?

14

Choices were made that did not include his welfare. Decisions were made that never considered a boy growing up without a mom, dad, or grandmother. What about the responsibility that falls on a young boy to take care of a great-grandmother when she is ill while others play outside and go to little league football games? What right was there for these adults to take away his childhood dreams and memories for their own selfish desires? What about this little boy who had to grow up way too fast without a choice? This is a real boy. He is not a character in a book or on a weekly TV show. Should his voice be heard?

What about the child who has called so many men "daddy" that he doesn't really know what it means. None of them seem to have his name, and they never seem to stay around very long. The word daddy comes naturally to young children because in every one of us is a built-in desire to have that position filled in our lives. This is a real story. As a matter of fact, this is a real story for more children than one. We know some of their names, but you probably do too in your community, at your school, or visiting your home. What about this child's voice? What about the others just like him?

How about the young lady whose daddy always promised to come by and take "daddy's little girl" out to the park or to a movie, or maybe out for a burger, but he never shows up. Sometimes there is a phone call with a sorry, but most of the time there is just silence until the next promised day and the cycle continues. He never arrives. He never keeps his promise. So she looks for love in all the wrong places trying to fill a void, that hollow place in her heart. The consequences for her are great and painful, for the love she seeks turns ugly when she places her heart in the wrong hands. There are consequences in her life for these decisions as she seeks for what is lost.

Whose fault is this? Is it hers, or is it her dad's? She is not even legal age. She is only a child. Ephesians 6:2 says, "Honor your father and mother–this is the first commandment with a promise." That promise is "that it may go well with you and that you will enjoy long life on this earth." How do you teach a child like this how to honor someone who has hurt her so deeply? Not once, or twice, but over and over again. Even deeper, how do you get her to understand the love of a Heavenly Father, Jesus, who desires to "lavish" His love upon her when she has such a distorted view of love? This too is a real story. Her voice will be heard.

These are all real stories of kid's lives. Most of their letters are in this book. They are not fictitious characters. They are alive and breathing, but for most of them, something is dead inside, something they feel only an earthly dad can fill. This book brings the truth of their lives to you, the reader, but also the hope that lies ahead for them through healing, forgiveness, and restoration.

This book houses not only the voices of these children, but hundreds of other children as well that I have watched cry out for their fathers. I want you to hear their hearts. Listen to what they have to say to their daddy. Some of them have never met their daddy. Some have and at times wish they hadn't because knowing him is too painful. Some know him, love him, live with him, and praise God for him. I wish this was every story, but it isn't. You will find these letters embedded among the others. They will come as a relief to your spirit. They will bring you joy and hope for what can be if it isn't already.

The "daddy letter" for many of these individuals was part of their healing process. Some of them are still walking out their healing and that is okay, too. Moving forward (even if it means you went three steps forward and then one back) is better than not moving anywhere at all. For some of these children, there is a final step that needs to take place and it includes their fathers. For some this is still possible. For others, circumstances such as death or legal separation for the safety of that child may prohibit such a step.

Voices

Are you that father? Are you the one they call daddy because they don't know you by any other name? Or maybe you are a child that needs to sit down and write your letter. Even if you never send it, or if it is never published in a book, write it and take that step towards healing.

These letters are not fabricated or created. These letters are written by real children, youth, and adults. I have them stored in a safe place to protect their names and their private lives. I have included their gender and ages for a reason. If I were to place a name on the page, you could not place your name there, and you just might need to do that in order to find your healing. You just might find yourself in one of these letters. Maybe you see your face on one of these pages. Maybe it is your story. Maybe, just maybe, you need time to cry out for yourself.

Maybe it is your child's story, and you are the one called "daddy" or the one who would be called daddy if you had stayed around. Your child may not have written the letter line by line, but you can picture his or her face on the page. As you read the letters, you will see that all of the children are not still young. They have grown up, but the pain is still there. Some grew up and want to share what it was like to have an awesome dad.

All of these voices need to be heard because they are a representation of the world in which we live. My world, your world, is impacted by these voices. These voices are heard every day in our school classrooms, on college campuses, on our job sites, in our hospitals, in psych wards, on baseball playing fields, in dance studios, at the mall, and in our churches. They are heard everywhere by the individual reactions people have to situations that occur in everyday life.

A reaction you get in the classroom or on the job site may have nothing to do with you or the situation at hand, but everything to do with what is bottled up inside, and when a wound is bumped, it usually bleeds. People are bleeding all over the place and the world is becoming a bloody mess. It is time to stop the bleeding.

It is time to silence the negative words that have been spoken over the lives of children, and maybe over your life as well. These words need to be cancelled. We need to be careful of what comes out of our mouth. Words penetrate a heart and can go deep into the soul of a precious girl, boy, woman, or man.

"The tongue has the power of life and death, and those who love it will eat its fruit." Proverbs 18:21

Some of the words spoken over the lives of the children in these letters and maybe over your life have produced bitter fruit that has given birth to anger, hatred, crime, lust, alcoholism, drug addiction and sickness, but some of the words spoken have brought life, and life abundantly. With these we rejoice.

Healing needs to come for both the wounded and for those who have inflicted wounds. Jesus sacrificed His life for people on both sides of the battle. The one who wins is the one who forgives and receives forgiveness. Rejoicing needs to be expressed by those who are able to rejoice in their relationships with their dads so others know they too can find rejoicing as healing comes. We don't want history to continue to repeat itself generation after generation. If you are reading this book, it is either your time to experience healing, or it is your time to understand those who are trying to find it.

Daddy, if you only knew…

"How I feel inside. It is so hard to grow up without a dad beside me, and you let me down so many times. I don't think that I can forgive you. If you say that you are going to do something for me, stick to what you say, and if something comes up, at least you can call me to let me know. Don't say that you are doing something with me, and you know that you can't do it. That is one thing that I hate."

12 Year Old Girl

Daddy, if you only knew…

"Dad, I wish you would stop playing the game, and you would play with me and play football with me and GET A JOB! Clean your room up, stop throwing things on the floor, and stop losing plates."

8 Year Old Boy

Daddy, If You Only Knew

Daddy, if you only knew...

"If you only knew how much pain you have caused, maybe you would not have made the decision that you made. Maybe if you knew how many nights I have laid awake just crying because of you. Maybe then you would have stopped drinking. Maybe you would have put it down. Dad, because of the decision you made to continue drinking, you have hurt me physically and emotionally. Because of that, I did not feel love from you. I felt like I had no self-worth and that I was ugly.

You never came to a practice or an event, and then when you did, I would mess up, and you would tell me I was wasting my time and needed to quit. Dad, I was so jealous of the neighborhood kids because they had their dads that supported and loved them and I didn't. Dad, when I would ask you to do something with me and my sister like play catch, you would always say NO, but as soon as someone else would ask you, you would.

I remember one night when you had got so drunk that you had lost your mind. My little sister cleaned out the fridge like you asked her to do, and she had accidentally thrown away the little bit of steak that you were planning to eat. When you found out, you got so mad that you threw a shoe at her and hit me instead. I was so ticked off that you threw a shoe at my sister, your youngest daughter! So I got up and told you that you needed to apologize and sit down. But you didn't care. You started going off on me. Then you grabbed my wrist, and I started yelling, screaming, and begging you to let go, but you didn't. I told my sister to get out, but she would not budge because she was too scared to move. Then you forced me to the ground, and I did not know what was going to happen to me next. All I knew was that I needed to grab the cell phone and get my sister out of there. As I was trying to get loose, you were telling me it was no use because I was weak and not good for anything. So I kicked you but it didn't work. I took your hand that was on my right side and hit it as hard as I could. You finally let me go and I grabbed the phone and got my sister out of there.

Dad, if you only knew how much I love you and pray for you, maybe this would have never happened."

19 Year Old Girl

Daddy, If You Only Knew

Daddy, if you only knew...

"Dear Daddy, if you only knew how much I cried, especially when you almost died. You were gone when I needed you most. You missed my only ballet recital. You told me I was fat and I had no friends, and now you are moving to another country and are going to miss everything. Why can't you just get a job in the States and stop causing problems when you're here and just be there when I need you?

When we get the little time we do together, STOP criticizing everything about me and just listen. STOP making it about you so you can get a chance to hear all the things you are missing like the very first time I sang in front of a big crowd, when I recorded my first CD, when I have a simple recital at church, or my induction to the 7th grade after jumping half a grade. Why can't you just...

SHUT UP AND LISTEN!

I can't tell you how much bitterness that I feel toward you that I just can't let go because you hurt me so bad. When the boys were punching me and hurting me, you shrugged your shoulders and said, 'Don't do it again,' so I had to learn to defend myself. Then you come around and act like nothing happened!"

12 Year Old Girl

Daddy, if you only knew...

"That I'm sad because you don't come to a church like my church. When you were in jail, you were talking about Jesus and things, but when you got out, you were just going to do right. But that just didn't happen.

You've been going your way. You've been coming home late. It seems like you don't care about us. Daddy, if you knew about Jesus, you would be going with Him. But you're not. I am talking to you about Him because you are not going on the right path."

12 Year Old Girl

Daddy, If You Only Knew

Daddy, if you only knew...

"Boy, it's been a long time since I've considered even writing a letter. How long has it been? I don't know, 14 to 15 years. There's something that I've always wanted to ask you. How come you don't want me? As a matter of fact, how come you didn't want me? Growing up was pointless kind of because as a child you don't know much. I remember when I was little, everything around me was suppose to be that specific way. One day it was a special day for fathers and I was clueless. It was Father's Day and I remember I was in Kindergarten. My teacher talked to all of us, saying that we should make a card for all our fathers or whatever. I, as a child, didn't know any better so I'd ask what a father was. My teacher said, "Your daddy". I was like, "I don't have one." All my little peers began to laugh. I'm like, "Why is everyone laughing at me?" Long story short, the teachers made all the kids in the class raise their hands that had a daddy. I was the only one who didn't raise my hand.

As years went by, that always bound me down because you were never there to see your son grow up. At the age of 11 my mom got married. I didn't like that because I would pray every night that you would get out of prison and come home. I basically prayed for 10 years, man. So ever since I was 7 years old, I've been praying for you even after mommy got married. Going to sleep crying, watching all my friends have a bond with their fathers. I felt like a drag along really, rejected a lot.

Well, at the age of 17 where I am now, things still are hard. It's even harder now because I am playing high school ball. While on the sideline when offense is on the field, I look back at the stands to see if you are there. When in reality I knew you aren't. After the game all my brothers on the team get dressed and walk out of the locker room. As I walk out of the locker room, I see all my boys hugging their dads and their dads telling them what a good job they did in the game. As for me, nothing happens.

It doesn't bother me as much as it used to. Somewhere deep inside I would have been much happier if I could have had that bond. There's a lot of jealousy in my heart because of rejection. I ain't even going to lie. Some nights I felt like I was an accident. There's 12 months in a year, 24 hours in a day and 7 days in a week. Imagine 365 days times 14 to 15, maybe even 16, years of rejection. I have lust in my heart because I was never taught the right way to love as a man. Mama can try to reach me all she wants to until she is blue in the face. Only a man can teach a man to be a man. Mama tried so long through those years. All it did for me was to go through one ear and out of the other ear. One day hopefully, I will become a father and have two beautiful kids with a beautiful and supportive wife. I am going to be the man you never were. It hurts me to say that, but I call it as I see it and lived it. There is some love for you and I forgive you."

17 year old boy

Daddy, If You Only Knew

Daddy, if you only knew...

"If you only knew how I needed you, and you were not there for me, but that is OK. I know that you don't love me. But that is OK. I know someone that does who will always be there when I call Him. He will not just up and leave, He will be there when I call Him. When I need someone or need help, He is always there. I am so happy you are not my father, Jesus is.

To tell you the truth, I do not want to become the man or father that you are. I hate you and I never want to see you again. You put me out of your life; now you are out of my life.

If you only knew my pastor who is a father when I need something although he does not always have it he will try to get it. You never even tried. When I need someone to talk to, he is always there. You were never there. You did not think about me. Jesus and father, they pray for me. I hate you so much.

Every day I try to become a better man. You should try that. Just to let you know, Jesus loves you and the world, but I hate you for real."

20 Year Old Male

Note to the reader: I struggled putting this letter in the book because of the intense anger that brought forth such strong feelings of hate. I know this young man, and he is walking through his healing. If your feelings bring forth hate, allow this book to walk you through your healing.

Chapter 2

Forgiveness

Chapter 2

FORGIVENESS

True healing can only come when true forgiveness occurs. If you are the child, you need to forgive your father no matter the circumstance. This does not make light of your pain or mean you have to "water down" the horror of the circumstance, it means it is time to help yourself by releasing your father into the hands of a living God and trust the Heavenly Father to take care of your inner healing. You do not have to honor what he did to you or how painful the circumstance might have been; it is the office he holds you must honor. This may seem like a huge mountain to climb, but if you have a relationship with your Heavenly Father, Jesus, you are not climbing this one alone. As a matter of fact, if you let Him, He will carry you all the way to the top, but you have to want to get there.

The message of honoring your father and mother is in the Word of God eight times. Exodus 20:12, Deuteronomy 5:16; Matthew 15:4, Matthew 19:19, Mark 7:10, Mark 10:19; Luke 18:20; Ephesians 6:2-3. Honor your father (mentioned first) and your mother -which is the first commandment with a promise- "that it may go well with you and that you may enjoy long life on the earth."

"Honor your father and your mother, ***so that you may live long in the land the LORD your God is giving you.*** " Exodus 20:12

He has land He has planned to give you from the beginning of time; it is your destiny. Don't let unforgiveness rob you of your land. That land may be the gifts that He has placed within you that are going to rise up and be released as you walk in forgiveness. That land may be a physical place or an abode. Don't limit God by tying His hands through your unforgiveness.

"For if you forgive men when they sin against you, your Heavenly Father will also forgive you. But if you do not forgive men their sins, your Father will not forgive your sins." Matthew 6:14-15

If you are the one called "daddy," and you know you have wounded your children, you need to ask God for forgiveness. Then you need to come to the place where you can ask your children for forgiveness. If this is not possible, which sometimes is the case, then know that God sees your heart. Secondly, you need to forgive yourself. Sometimes this mountain is harder than asking others to forgive us, but God's desire is to make us whole, and complete forgiveness is the only thing that sears shut our bleeding wounds. We will explore this in more detail later on in this book, but if you feel the Spirit of God speaking to you right now, don't let the moment pass without praying this very simple prayer.

Forgiveness

For the Child who needs to forgive:

"Father God, I have had my heart broken by my earthly father. Right now, this very moment, I ask You to help me to release this hold I have on my father by carrying around this pain, hurt, bitterness, and disappointment in my heart. I choose this day to forgive my father. I release him, therefore releasing myself from anger, fear, low self-esteem, and bitterness."

For the Dad who needs to ask for forgiveness:

"Father God, I have broken the heart of my child. I have wounded (him/her/them), and I am asking that You forgive me for not taking my place in (his/her/their) life. Heal their heart(s) as You are healing mine."

For the Dad who needs to forgive himself:

"Father God, when I look into my own heart it feels impossible to forgive myself for the pain I have caused my children. Right now, I ask You to help me to forgive myself for what I have done. I ask You to help my children to forgive me as I seek their forgiveness. I ask You to help me within my own heart to become the godly father You have called me to be, even if it is not physically possible for me to ever personally reach my children."

By saying these prayers, the healing balm has begun in your heart. Balm is an ointment that soothes and heals. The Holy Spirit is that balm, that comforter you need right now. He is the one Jesus promised would come as a gift to comfort us after he ascended back to the throne of God following His

31

resurrection. Linger in His presence and receive all that God has for you. Sometimes healing is a lengthy process of breaking through one barrier at a time. Sometimes it is a quick work. Trust your Heavenly Father to complete the work that has just begun.

Daddy, if you only knew...

"Thank you for being there for me. If you only knew what I am going through every single day, screaming, and doing some other bad stuff. I wish (you) my Daddy never did this stuff, but it is teaching me not to do the dad (bad) stuff."

10 Year Old Girl

Forgiveness

Dear Dad,

"If you only knew about the seemingly endless river of
anger inside of me. Everyone thinks I have it "all together"
on the outside, yet underneath, I am the girl you physically
and emotionally abused for years. When I confronted you
with the truth of my childhood, you ran from it in pride.
You did not apologize for what you did to me. You hid
under false pretenses and self preservation. I pray that the
Lord removes the veil from your heart and your mind, so
that one day you can repent to Him and to me. When you
mess with unrepentance, you are playing with fire, Dad. For
a man reaps what he sows. I pray to the Lord to have mercy
on you all of the time.

The Lord is healing my river of anger and replacing it with
His liquid love for me. I know I am His daughter, highly
favored and loved just because I am me. Father God fills
the void left by you Dad. You required obedience and
perfection at all costs. Father God accepts me for who I am
and loves me into obedience.

Dad, you are old now. I hope that someday soon you will
realize that you could have blessed instead of cursed; you
could have caused laughter instead of tears; you could have
provoked love instead of anger.

Anger is dangerous. I turned the anger inward for many
years and did not hurt others, but only myself. I had
suffered from anxiety, depression, and some chronic health

problems. As I forgive and bless you, the Lord grants me peace and health. The devil no longer has a foothold to torment my body or my mind. In fact, the abuse I suffered at your hand will be redeemed many times over as I minister to others who have also been abused. I cannot wait to usher others into this freedom that now I am beginning to walk out.

Dad, you made your choice. You remain hardened, still verbally abusing my mom. I made my choice. I am not controlled by your anger anymore. Strength has replaced my fear as I have drawn healthy boundaries around myself when it comes to dealing with you. There is no wall around my heart anymore, only a protective hedge around me and my family in which you can not enter in. The choice is yours. I will not give up hope that your pride will crumble someday, and maybe then you will be the dad and grandpa that you were called to be."

Chosen Daughter of God,
Kim

Forgiveness

Daddy, if you only knew...

"That the most important thing in a girl's life is her father. With importance comes a foundation, an example of how life will look. I wanted so bad to run home after school and tell you and mom about my day, to feel that embrace. You were never there. You destroyed mother, and when you hurt and abused her, I was lost because you were supposed to be the protector, my Knight in shining armor.

I wanted a father to love, hold, hug, and play with. One to run to when I was scared, confused, and needed a lap to curl up on and a shoulder to cry on. I would have loved to hear the words "You're special," "I love you," "You're my little princess," "You are so beautiful, just like the sunrise." Those words I did not hear, and I began to live in fear, afraid of what would happen when you sent me away, what would happen when you went to jail for abusing me, stripping my innocence from me. If you only knew how much I cried and then stayed up afraid to close my eyes. How all I wanted was to be anywhere but with you. Know that I have found God. I have a Heavenly Father, one who was everything you weren't. I wish you could have done the things that He did. He picked me up when I fell down. He wiped my tears and fears away. He protected me and made me feel worth something.

Daddy, I only wish that you had been there for me at anytime in my life. A part of me hates you for what you did, and other parts of me forgives you and wants you to take a second chance and do it right."

19 Year Old Female

Daddy, If You Only Knew

Dear Dad,

"I didn't know you long. I met you when I was about 2;
you adopted me to have your last name. You taught me
so much, like how to swim and water ski when I was 3.
You had big muscles and loved to work out and run. I
thought you were the strongest man in the world! My
mom and you argued a lot, and I'd lie in bed and hear all
the screaming and fighting and wish it would stop.

One day when I was 5, mom woke me up and asked me
if I knew what divorce was. I didn't and you two gave
me a book about divorce. That morning I was asked who
I wanted to live with and I said my mom, but it was
so hard to pick. I ended up with my grandmother, and
you would come in your Trans Am to take me to soccer
games and out to eat. Your job eventually moved you
state to state so you wrote me a lot. When my cousin told
me you weren't my real father why did you want nothing
to do with me? I was only 12, and even though you
weren't my real dad, you were all I ever knew. The next
and last time I heard from you I was 20, and because I
had a mixed son at the time, you couldn't accept him, so
I said you couldn't accept me either. I'm now 37 years old
with two mixed boys, and we love God.

I wish you would have stayed in my life. My sons are so
wonderful and I didn't turn out so bad either."

37 Year old Female

36

Forgiveness

Daddy, if you only knew...

"That I love you with all my heart, and that sometimes I can't stand you. I tell myself sometimes that you aren't my Daddy because a real father would realize that he's hurting his family by the things he's doing. Daddy, to me it seems not a day comes that you don't do that. Daddy, if you only knew how much I want you to get saved. I'm tired of you smoking in the house, being lazy, not cleaning up behind yourself and expecting us (your kids) to clean it up.

There were many times I asked the Lord to forgive me just for saying that I hate you. I am so scared to tell you about Jesus because I think that you're not going to listen and reject me. Daddy, if you only knew I would do anything just for you and mama to come to church and listen to what the pastor says. One more thing, if you would just embrace me with a hug and say that you love me."

16 year old Girl

Daddy if you only knew...

"How I felt about you years ago compared to how I feel about you now. The Lord has done such healing between us because we both have chosen to let the past die and the new day come forth. Since I was 19 years old, you have become my best friend. Because of travel, I see you less now than I did back then, but whenever I call you, it is as if we just were together yesterday. Dad, I have seen the Lord restore our relationship and also our entire heritage through your faithfulness and dedicated prayers. God has promised this to our family several years ago, and the Lord has indeed finally done such a great and magnificent work! Thank you, Dad, for sticking with Christ when everything around you over the years could have told you otherwise. Your efforts have changed all of our lives."

"He will call out to me, 'You are my Father, my God, the Rock my Savior.'" Psalm 89:26

Andy Sanders, age 35

Chapter 3

Perfect Love Drives out Fear

Chapter 3

PERFECT LOVE DRIVES OUT FEAR

I asked children ages six to fourteen what they feared the most would hinder their success and their dreams for the future. All sorts of fears were expressed. I had them write them down anonymously so I could pray over them. I still have them. They are stored in the same safe place as the "Daddy letters." This is what they said:

"I am afraid my parents are going to get a divorce and my dad will move."
"I am afraid my dad might die early because he is doing drugs."
"I am afraid because of my family."
"I am afraid because I do not have a dad."
"I am afraid that my dad's mistakes might hold me back."
"I am afraid of my dad dying from cigarettes."
"My dad is poor."
"I am worried about my mom getting killed."
"I am most feared of family."
"I have a bad family."

"I think that my family is bad because I don't have money for a good car."

"I am afraid my father will not get out of jail."

"I am afraid of being rejected and not fitting in."

"I have no identity anywhere or in anything I do."

"I am stupid/dumb."

"I will never pass in school."

"I am afraid I will never go to college."

"I am poor."

"I am afraid of not having any money."

"I am afraid of stealing money."

"I am afraid of getting in a car crash and dying and not succeeding in my dreams."

"I am afraid of dying."

"I am afraid of sickness."

Do you see reoccurring themes here? A lot of their fears revolved around the possibility of losing their dads, their moms, or the impact of what they called "bad family members." They had fear of failure, sickness, death, and the results of their looming poverty. This is sometimes caused by single parent homes, and the lack of faithful child support from a former spouse or partner. Sometimes poverty resulted from the absence of both parents leaving them to be raised by elderly grandparents living on a fixed income. Without a secure environment and continual reassurance of love from a committed adult, they were consumed with all kinds of fear. As parents, we pave the way for our children. Our positioning can open doors or close doors for our children. In other words, our actions can bring blessing or cursing on our children. We have got to evaluate our decisions in relation to their impact on our children's lives. In our culture, we are identified by the name we carry, and if that name has a bad history, children can carry it in the terms of fear.

Perfect Love Drives Out Fear

I have good news! Father God's love for you fights all fear. His love drives it out. His love hates fear. His love destroys fear. His love damages the work the enemy (Satan) intended fear to play in your life. His love is perfect and perfect love drives out fear. The Word of God says, "There is no fear in love. But perfect love drives out fear, because fear has to do with punishment. The one who fears is not made perfect in love" 1 John 4:18. You don't have to be a slave to it any longer. When you come into a real relationship with Jesus, He calls you son or daughter and you can call Him "Abba" or Daddy.

"For you did not receive a spirit that makes you a slave again to fear, but you received the Spirit of sonship. And by Him we cry, *"Abba* (Daddy) Father" Romans 8:15.

But if you should choose not to accept His love for you this day, know that His love for you has nothing to do with your love for Him. He is love and He will continue to love you unconditionally. That is what godly fathers do. What do you have to lose by accepting His love except your fears? It just takes a little faith. Faith and love are inseparable. As you step out in faith to believe and receive Father God as your personal and real Savior, Father God Himself pours, pours, and pours His love into you.

"How great is the love the Father has **lavished** on us, that we should be called children of God! And that is what we are!" I John 3:1

This is our hope and it does not disappoint. Even if you do not have a good frame of reference on what a godly father should look like, take a leap of faith and place your hope in Father God. This is the hope that I offer every child I meet if given the opportunity, and today I offer it to you.

Yes, even you, the daddy that maybe feels he failed. God wants to lavish His love on you. There is no greater teacher of a father's love than Father God.

Prayer for Hope and Release from Fear

"Father God, I recognize that I need hope and that You are the only hope. I also realize that You are love and that Your love is perfect. It is perfect to cast out any fear that I have. Would you take away my fear and replace it with hope once again?"

With fear gone it opens up the possibility for you to dream BIG again! To dream beyond where anyone in your natural family may have gone or anything they may have accomplished. To believe once again that you can fulfill your dreams and not be crippled by fear.

For the children we worked with, the ones who wrote these letters, the only thing that could help them broaden their dreams was who they chose to place their hope in. When your hope is in Father God, all that He has is available to you and He only wants what is best for His children. The challenge came when I used the words Heavenly Father, because ninety percent of the kids I was working with had little to no reference to the word father or at best a negative reference to that word. Maybe this is your story too. Maybe this is why you have trouble understanding or relating to a God that is called Father.

I desperately wanted these children to understand HOPE; a hope in something bigger than their frame of reference; a hope in a Heavenly Father, Jesus, who would never bail out on them. They wouldn't wake up one morning and Him not be there or lay in bed hearing fighting and screaming, wishing He would just disappear. When children or youth

44

call me crying, telling me that they hate their life, I always remind them that this is their present life because of the choices being made by the adults they are submitted to as a minor. I tell them to look ahead into the future. With a new-found hope in Jesus, their future can look drastically different when the life's choices become their own as adults. It is a challenge sometimes trying to keep children encouraged caught in life's perils due to parental choices, while being very careful not to disrespect the adults in their lives because they still needed to respect and honor them.

Maybe you have lost the ability to dream due to things that have happened in your life or maybe you feel inhibited by finances. Your dream costs money to accomplish and money has never been available. Don't stop dreaming. God owns it all! He has big dreams for you, too! He is just waiting for you to start walking in what He has already destined for you.

"For I know the plans I have for you," declares the Lord, "plans to prosper you and not to harm you, plans to give you hope and a future." Jeremiah 29:11

The bottom line is that Father God loves YOU! When He looks at you, He sees something He loves. Nothing you do can change His love for you! It is His absolute nature to love you. He cannot love you more or less than He already does. It is not about what you have done or not done. It is a love that is unconditional.

Even after knowing the Lord for over forty years, I came to a new revelation of this love and the true depth of it. It came through a song I heard while waiting on Him for our next direction, our next purpose in this amazing Kingdom of God. This song played over and over again, a song called "Inheritance" by Jonathan David Helser and Graham Cooke.

He is our inheritance. I could not move forward until I truly realized how much He loves me, and that I was set free to be me.

He loves you so much that He wants to set you free from yourself, for you can only love Him as you learn to love yourself. He wants to set you free from low self-esteem, from rejection of any kind, from abuse, and from the lack of belief in yourself. ***Will you let Him love you as a Father?***

Daddy, if you only knew...

"Daddy, I love you. You are so special to me. You make me feel so happy. You buy a lot of stuff for me. Sometimes you break my heart. You are like a bear to me. When I hug you, you feel so soft. I cannot stop thinking about you because you mean so much to me. Sometimes you scare me when you get mad, like a cat, because you have a mean face. And when you get mad, you hurt my heart."

Daddy's girl,
9 Year Old Girl

Daddy, if you only knew...

"My only best Daddy is God, but I love the one that is taking care of me. These are the best daddy's I ever had. I want to go to Orlando and wish I knew better about you Jesus."

12 Year Old Girl

Daddy, if you only knew…

"I will love and hug you! Daddy, I wish I knew you and could see you. Then you could come to church with me. Also, we could go places together like you could take me to practice and watch me. Also, you can see how God is in my life! I have something I would like to ask you! If you loved me, why didn't you stay out of jail so I can get to know you? I am 15 and only seen you 2 times. Daddy, I know I don't know you and it hurts to know that you are dying of AIDS. I never got to know you! I still love you even though you hurt me, and have never been there for me! Yes! I forgive you but don't forget how much you hurt me! Daddy, I do pray for God to heal you and you come to know God! I LOVE YOU!"

15 Year Old Boy

Daddy, if you only knew…

"How much I love you no matter what may happen. I still have hope in you that you may have understanding in everything you do, and even if you don't really understand, I won't give up on you. You help me through these menacing days of my life.

Daddy, if you only knew that you help me each and every day although you may not notice it. I do and that's what matters. You taught me how to love everyone else besides me. If you are too afraid to talk to anyone, talk to Jesus because everything's going to be all right, just believe.

Daddy, if you only knew that, you might change only for the better, but I won't stop loving you because I won't change anything about myself that will affect you in anyway. You are my light that shines on me and gives me strength.

Daddy, if you only knew that you give me joy, love, adoring moments, and most of all you give me life. Dad, I love you more than I can say, and you should know, so I guess I can say I love you.

Daddy, if you only knew how much I love you."

13 Year Old Girl

Daddy, if you only knew...

"Father, every day I lived I haven't seen you, and it hurts so bad I wish you could see me but you can't see me. At first I thought you did not love me at all, but then God said he would be my Father so I forgive you. I love you to death, even though you were never there. I wish you could see how I've grown, what I love to do. You don't know because you were never there. I wish you could see me. You don't know that every day I go to school I tell my friends that my father is dead, and I fear that is the truth, but I forgive you, Father."

Girl, age unknown

Daddy, if you only knew...

"Daddy, I don't really know if you are _____ or _____ but it don't matter now because you are both dead. Never really met you before. Wish I did. Sometimes I think you were not really a good example. I used to feel sad because I thought I had no daddy until I heard about my Heavenly Father. I wish you could have been there for me to be the father I needed. I wish I knew you and we had a closer relationship as father and daughter. I live with my mom's mom because she gave me away to my grandma because I was too noisy as a baby. Now I am bigger and I asked to live with my mom, but grandma says I need to stay with someone who really takes care of me and appreciate that because I could have been a foster child. I am glad that my Heavenly Father eases my pain and dries my tears when I wonder who my dad is and I know that I have a Father who is always there. I wish I could see you."

Your daughter,

12 1/2 Year Old Girl

Daddy, If You Only Knew

Daddy, if you only knew…

"That I am on a SWAT (Leadership Ministry) Team. Then I think, NO, you do not know that because you do not choose to see me any day. If you want to know, I am ok without you. I love Jesus. Do you? You should come with me to church.

I guess you are so busy so you will not come to see me, anyway. So do not come to see me. OK? I love my God. Do you love God? Just say yes. I love you Dad. All my best to you. Know that and you are always in my heart. I love you."

13 Year Old Boy

Daddy, if you only knew…

"I love you! I miss you! I want you to get out of jail and buy me some clothes and shoes. I want you to take me some places. I want you to take me to Busch Gardens. I have dreams of you and me going somewhere and my sisters running to us. Daddy's girl."

7 Year Old Girl

Chapter 4

No Orphans in the Kingdom

NO ORPHANS
IN THE KINGDOM

God is a "Father to the fatherless." Psalm 68:5

America has vastly become a fatherless nation. According to the Fatherhood Foundation, children without fathers in the home are:
- 32 times more likely to run away.
- 5 times more likely to commit suicide.
- 9 times more likely to drop out of high school.
- 2.5 times more likely to become a teen parent, potentially repeating the cycle.
- 37 times more likely to abuse drugs.
- twice as likely to live in poverty.
- twice as likely to commit a crime.

The National Fatherhood Initiatives cited the following facts:
- 24 million children (34%) live absent from their biological father.
- 1.35 million births (33 percent of all births) in 2000 occurred out of wedlock.
- about 40% of children living absent from their fathers

have not seen their fathers at all during the past year.
- 26% of absent fathers live in a different state than their children.
- 50% of children living absent from their fathers have never stepped a foot in their home.

This looks pretty grim, but this does not take into the consideration the truth of the Kingdom of God operating in the heart of a child committed solely to Daddy Jesus.

God does not have any orphans in His Kingdom. If you do not have a physical daddy active in your life, stop telling people you don't have a daddy. You have a Daddy. When you accept Jesus Christ as Lord and Savior, you are adopted as sons and daughters of the Living God. And when you are adopted, you get all the rights given a son and daughter. WOW!

In any given setting, there are probably at least one or two people who can quote *The Lord's Prayer* from memory, even if they don't believe it to hold any significance in their life. The odds are very high that you, reading this book, can quote most of it, if not all of it, from memory. It starts out "Our Father." That means we have the amazing opportunity to be called children of God. When we accept the truth of who Jesus really is, even if we have not ever known an earthly father, we are no longer "fatherless." *The Lord's Prayer* holds another great revelation. It says in Matthew 6:10, "Your Kingdom come, Your will be done **on earth as it is in heaven.**" We are to believe and pray for the spiritual presence and manifestation (meaning to display, show, or demonstrate) of the Kingdom of God here on earth **NOW!**

According to His Word, Hebrews 11:13, talking about the great men of faith in the Bible like Abraham, Isaac, Jacob, Moses, and many others, says, "And they admitted that they were **aliens** and strangers on earth." As we become great men (boys) and women (girls) of faith by asking Jesus to take reign and rule in our lives, we too become aliens and strangers on earth. According to Matthew 6:10, we are not supposed to live in an earthly realm and "visit" the heavenly realm every once and a while. We are to live in the heavenly realm (Thy Kingdom come on earth as it is in heaven) and visit the earthly realm with His manifested presence. The Kingdom of God is God expressing Himself powerfully in ALL HIS WORKS through humanity. He expresses Himself through His children, adopted sons and daughters of God, no matter what their age.

If we can teach a child this revelation, they just might be able to survive in a place that feels like a virtual hell because they have learned how to "seek first the Kingdom of God" and their vision will become supernatural instead of natural. The problem is most of us adults haven't understood this revelation from Matthew 6:10. We have accepted Jesus as the Lord over our lives, but we have either forgotten, or maybe we have not fully understood that He is a supernatural God residing in the hearts of mere man. That means we are to live supernatural lives.

"But you are a chosen people, a royal priesthood, a holy nation, a people belonging to God, that you may declare the praises of Him who *called you out of darkness into His wonderful light."* I Peter 2:9

Most children understand the Star Wars story line or something similar, and us "older children" understand Star Trek. We know those famous lines like "Beam me up, Scotty." At that moment, in an instant, Captain Kirk is translated from one place to another.

Maybe you relate more to the Matrix world. Morpheus and Neil could represent the Christian walk. When they make a decision to leave the world as it appears and are translated from one world to another (from the good to the bad), they are translated from darkness into light. They know they have the truth and are willing to die for it if need be. They have made a choice to not live a life of duplication represented by what the world has to offer, a world where everyone talks about individuality as an excuse to look and act exactly like those around him. That is a sad natural world.

Oh, for our precious children, our fatherless kids to realize that upon receiving Christ as their Heavenly Daddy they have been translated (immediately transported into a new place) from darkness into His wonderful light. They are a new creation. Upon receiving Christ into their lives, they are translated into a supernatural life. They can now partake with the divine nature of God.

If they could grasp this simple yet complex truth, maybe their sight (perception and perspective) would supernaturally change, and they would go from survival mode in the natural to success mode in the supernatural. Just maybe they would begin to believe enough in themselves because of what their Heavenly Father says about them that it cancels the negative words and situations around them, even when those "speaking" are called father or mother, mommy or daddy.

I realize that this seems like an "ideal" dream, but it comes right from the heart of Father God who loves children, and who loves YOU! You are important and significant to God and the workings of His Kingdom here on earth today! Children and youth can offer hope to each other because they actually talk and listen to each other.

"Believe me when I say that I am in the Father and the Father is in Me; or at least believe on the evidence of the miracles themselves. I tell you the truth, ***anyone who has faith in Me will do what I have been doing. He will do even greater things*** than these, because I am going to the Father. And I will do whatever you ask in My name, so that the Son may bring glory to the Father." John 14:11-13

As we begin to operate in the heavenly realm, actually believing His Word, we bring Him glory. All that our "Daddy" Jesus did He says we can do. There are no orphans in the Kingdom of God, just people who have not realized all of their rights as adopted sons and daughters.

How is this possible? The only way to move in a supernatural realm is to spend time loving a supernatural God. Prayer is essential. Loving God is essential. Eating from His banqueting table in His Word is essential. A child can do this. I have seen it in the middle of what some called the "hood," but what we called beautiful.

I have seen God move upon children where they began to dance demonstratively before Him, unchoreographed, completely abandoned before Him with no dance like the other one. It could not be learned behavior because they had no religious history to pull from. Some of us need to ask God to erase some of our religious history so we can see clearly in the supernatural realm what He is doing in the body and world today.

Some reading this book walked away from a relationship with Father God years ago because of religion. God hates religion. He loves relationship. He loves you. You were created to commune with Him. He loves being with you. He longs to be with you! He will never love you more or less than He loves you today because He already loves you to the fullest, which means He loves you unconditionally, one hundred percent.

His love has nothing to do with your ability or lack of ability to love Him back. It has nothing to do with how good you are or how bad you are. It has nothing to do with where you come from or what neighborhood you live in. He loves you so much and He created you in His image. You are His favorite. It is time to start living as children of God.

Mark Chapter 5 speaks of a synagogue ruler named Jarius who came to seek Jesus to come and pray for his daughter who was very sick. While he was waiting to speak with Jesus, men came from his house and said that his daughter had died. They told Him to not "bother" Jesus anymore. Jesus then said in Mark 5:39 that "The child is not dead but asleep." In verse 41, Jesus spoke these words, "Talitha Koum" which means "Little girl I say to you get up." Then she got up and walked around. Jesus is saying the same to this fatherless generation that have been wounded and are bleeding. Some are facing spiritual death, and some facing possible physical death because of the bitterness and anger that is literally killing their physical body. God says to them; He is saying to you, ***"Talitha Koum, Get up and live."***

Daddy, if you only knew...

"I wish you knew the Lord and that we can be a family all again and that you will stop what you are doing and come to church so you can get to go to heaven with me. You are the one for me. God loves you, but you have sins in your heart and God can wash them out and make your heart clean."

13 year old Girl

Daddy, if you only knew…

"Let me tell you a story about how my father came from good to bad. My father was a good man but drugs and alcohol made him think of others and not his kids. My father sells drugs and drinks beer. So people say, "how does it feel to have a father leave when you were young?" It felt bad because when I was young, he was not there.

When I am older I hope my father will be there for my basketball games."

12 Year Old Girl

Daddy, if you only knew...

"Daddy if you only knew that my heart is unfulfilled without you. If you only knew that I need you. As of now I've done so much bad that there's only little good. If you only knew that I come to church to find some hope. Without you in my life it is incomplete. If you only knew that at your funeral I forced myself to cry because I didn't know you, so I couldn't. You are a complete stranger in my life.

I only wish that you'd done right by my mother that she wouldn't have left you. I wish I could have spent time with you that I could know you emotionally and spiritually. If you only knew that I look to the wrong people for love. I shall only thank you for life."

13 year old Girl

Daddy, if you only knew...

"That I really want to see you, be in your life, and live with you. I just want to see you so much. I love you and I want to see where you live and where you work at. I wish that I could come down there and see you. Thank you for being in touch when I was little. Thank you for being in my life. Thank you for buying me stuff and just loving me back."

9 year Old Girl

Daddy, if you only knew...

"How I feel. I feel sad and upset because you are not here. If you were here we could go to the park and play together. We could go on vacation together to Busch Gardens. I want my other side of the family to be with me too, like my brothers and sisters. I feel like someone is missing."

10 Year Old Girl

Daddy, if you only knew...

"I wish that you would live with me for the rest of my life. You have been very nice and sweet to me since I was a very little girl.

I haven't seen you in a while. I feel sad when I don't see you. Every time you do something nice it makes me very happy with you. I just wish it were more often.

Sometimes when I think about you I cry all day. I will always love you forever and ever and ever!"

From your daughter,
7 Year Old Girl

Daddy, if you only knew...

"Daddy, I know you want to be with me. I know you give me nice things, but now I have a new daddy. I'm so sad that you are not there for me, but I want to see my other sister and brother for the last time and visit you one more time before I forget."

10 year old Boy

Daddy, if you only knew...

"How I felt when my mom told me that you wasn't even there when she was having my two brothers or wasn't there when I was born. How can you even live with yourself? Why are you telling people that you don't have kids and then come back to us and say you love us, when you don't? That night when I was crying, I wasn't crying because I wanted to see you, I was crying because you broke my heart."

11 Year Old Girl

Chapter 5

Children are of Utmost Importance to God

CHILDREN ARE OF UTMOST
IMPORTANCE TO GOD

Let's examine the Word and see God's heart for children.

"Sitting down, Jesus called the Twelve and said, 'If anyone wants to be first, he must be the very last, and the servant of all.' He took a little child and had him stand among them. Taking him in His arms, He said to them, 'Whoever welcomes one of these little children in My name welcomes Me; and whoever welcomes Me does not welcome Me but the one who sent Me.'" Mark 9:35-37

When we welcome a child, we not only welcome "Daddy" Jesus but also God the Father. **Mark 10:13-15** says, "People were bringing little children to Jesus to have Him touch them, but the disciples rebuked them. When Jesus saw this, He was indignant. He said to them, 'Let the little children come to me, and do not hinder them, for the Kingdom of God belongs to such as these. I tell you the truth, anyone who will not receive the Kingdom of God like a little child will never enter it.'"

Daddy, If You Only Knew

My husband and I reopened a church in a very impoverished community completely by faith with no salary and no natural way of paying for the 11,000 square foot building. God told us there was a remnant in that community that was going to serve Him no matter what, and that we would find them among the children first and we did. God Himself targeted the children. He told us not to turn them away. We didn't, and they came, and they came, and they came.

The local newspaper said that "Nothing good comes out of this community." People told us to leave the children alone. They said, "There is no money in children and you need money." I don't see Jesus neglecting the children in Mark 10, and it is not what He said to us when we first walked in that dilapidated building. We found that remnant and God brought in the money because we dared to believe Him.

This remnant, these children and youth, learned to serve, preach, teach, lay hands on the sick and see them recovered. They learned to dance, act, perform in the art of puppetry, and then rise up as leaders wherever they went. They ran the children's ministry as children. My husband and I placed the ministry in their hands when we resigned. Some of them are a bit taller, older, and wiser than when they first began, but something was birthed in them early because we dared to believe, mentor, and spiritually parent them to do the work of the ministry as a child, or as a youth. We did not send them away for Jesus did not send them away.

God's desire is for us to enter the Kingdom of God NOW. Bring His manifested presence here on earth as it is in Heaven. Children will accept the Kingdom of God in a simple, humble, trustful manner, with their whole hearts so as to turn from their sin (which I refer to as a big three-letter word that most children do not understand. I describe it as all that bad stuff that does not line up with God's Word) and receive Him as their Lord and Savior.

Child-like Prayer to Receive Jesus as Your Heavenly Father and Savior:

"Jesus, I ask that You come into my heart and forgive me of all that bad stuff that stuff you call sin, that I have done that does not line up with God the Father's Word. I choose today, not tomorrow, but today, to make You the Lord of my life. That means to make You number one in every area of my life, not number 2, not number 3, but number one. In Jesus' name. Amen!"

If you said this prayer and you meant it in your heart, you are now a child of the King of all Kings. At this very moment you may feel you have much time wasted, but God is about to repay you for lost years.

"I will repay you for the years the locusts have eaten...and you will praise the name of the Lord your God, who has worked wonders for you; never again will my people be shamed." Joel 2:25-27

Daddy, If You Only Knew

Daddy, if you only knew...

"How special I felt when you took me to the park or to a movie when I was young and it was just me and you.

How when I was sick in the middle of the night and needed medicine you went to get it without hesitation no matter how late it was.

How scary it was when you went out on a call as the Fire Marshal and mom got a call that you were badly hurt. You had broken your back. Life as we knew it would forever be changed, but thanks to your reassurances and your hard work at getting better, we always had a roof over our head and food in our bellies. You went from being Fire Marshal of Tampa to being a bridge tender and although things did change–what didn't change was the fact that I was safe. I was never hungry or homeless and you were always there being the head of the household.

How scared and uncomfortable I was when you and mommy yelled at each other"

46 year old Female

Daddy, if you only knew...

"I never knew how fun my dad was. He spoiled me because I'm good. I earn the goodness that my dad gives me, but I thank him for all his love he gives me. He loves me like I love him, when I do something wrong he forgives me."

10 Year Old Girl

Daddy, if you only knew...

"Let me tell you how I feel. I love you very much and you love me. I pray for you because you care for me, giving me shoes, clothes, and everything I need."

10 Year Old Girl

Daddy, if you only knew…

"You have always been there for me. Sometimes, I get mad at you but I get over it. Thank you for being there for me. When I am mad you cheer me up. If we have a play at school and I don't see you in the crowd, I know you want to be there even though you are not and I know you still love me.

Dad, this is how you are there for me like when you are doing something and my skate or something broke, you stop what you were doing and fixed it or when I needed you, you came."

12 Year Old Girl

Daddy, if you only knew…

"Thank you for being there for me. I love you! Thank you that when you were not there for my birthday, you make it back up to me or call me and say happy birthday. Thank you for loving me."

12 Year Old Girl

Daddy, if you only knew...

"Thank you for being in my life. I like the way you play with me. Thank you for being my dad."

13 Year Old Girl

Daddy, if you only knew...

"I love my mom and my dad. Thank you for buying me clothes and dresses, heels, and t-shirts, shoes, and I thank you for my life. I just want you to know that I am glad you are in my life."

6 Year Old Girl

Daddy, If You Only Knew

Daddy if you only knew...

"How much I love you. You were the best dad and always there when I needed you. You did a great job as a father, for not having your dad around to show you how to be a dad and how to be a man. I am sorry that your dad was never around for you when you were growing up. I'm glad you invited Jesus into your life when you were in your early 30's. You would pray and ask Him to show you how to be a father to us kids.

I know that it was God who helped you be the best dad for each of us kids. Thank you for spending time with us, taking us places with you without the others sometimes and treating us special when we were around you.

Thank you for taking us on father/daughter dates and I'm sure the boys would thank you for taking them on father/son dates.

Thank you for listening to God on how to be the best dad you could be for us."

38 Year Old Female

Children are of Utmost Importance to God

Daddy, if you only knew…

"How much you mean to me. I know you are not a very verbal person so words don't come easily for you, especially when it deals with personal and emotional things. As a child I may not have heard "I love you" or "I am proud of you" everyday, but you certainly showed these things in your actions. I remember how you used to tuck me in every night with a back scratch and a kiss on the forehead. Mom told me that as a baby you would rub my back as I lay in my crib every night to help me go to sleep.

You also are very conservative with money to make sure we had the things we needed. Even on a moderate income, you worked hard to save money for me to go to college without having to pay my own tuition.

One of the things I am most thankful for is that you brought me up in church, but more than that, you taught me that salvation is my own and not just an extension of your beliefs. In hard times, you taught me to trust God and not to doubt or question His plans. Fifteen years ago when my only brother passed away so suddenly at age 22, you didn't waiver, run, turn your back, or blame God for what happened. Those things weren't even an option. Thank you for that. You and mom showed me that trusting God is a lifestyle. Thank you for being a true example and for being there for me."

I love you Dad,
Cathy, 34 years old

Chapter 6

The Hearts of the Fathers

THE HEARTS OF THE FATHERS

I believe in these last days, God is calling the hearts of the fathers back to their children. I believe this book carrying the **voices of the children** to the hearts of the fathers is part of that move.

Zechariah was visited by an angel of the Lord with a very important message. We need to listen to this message today. The word reads in **Luke 1:12–17,** "When Zechariah saw him (the angel of the Lord), he was startled and was gripped with fear. But the angel said to him: 'Do not be afraid, Zechariah; your prayer has been heard. Your wife Elizabeth will bear you a son, and you are to give him the name John. He will be a joy and delight to you, and many will rejoice because of his birth, for he will be great in the sight of the Lord. He is never to take wine or other fermented drink, and he will be filled with the Holy Spirit even from birth. Many of the people of Israel will he bring back to the Lord their God. And he will go on before the Lord, in the spirit and power of Elijah, to turn the **hearts of the fathers to their children** and the disobedient to the wisdom of the righteous-**to make ready a people prepared for the Lord.**' "

Daddy, If You Only Knew

One of the greatest sins of God's people in the Old Testament was the fathers' failure to love their sons and daughters enough to teach them God's ways. Does that not sound like our world today? With the coming of John the Baptist, who pointed to Jesus the Messiah, the hope then is our hope today that the hearts of the fathers turn back to their children and they **NOW** begin to point their children to the Messiah. It is time for the fathers of this fatherless generation to rise up and seek first His Kingdom and His righteousness and write these principles upon their hearts and the hearts of their children in true repentance. Heavenly Father, please *let it begin with the voices of the children no longer being silenced.*

The voices in the letters housed in this book have not been silenced. As you can see, we have barely and minimally checked for good grammar and spelling. We did not coax anyone with what to say, for then it would not be their heart speaking, but ours. Some of it is harsh and you may think they should not have been allowed to write in this manner. These are their words as they wrote them.

But even through their pain, many of these children offer their earthly fathers unconditional love. Many of them desire good things for their fathers and long to be with them even if their experiences have not been good. Even if they have never met them or have known them by name. You see, children give forgiveness more freely than most adults. That is why a child will continually offer defense and love for an abusive parent or for a neglectful parent, yet many adults can't forgive what happened at the office or a church social among those whom they call friends. No wonder God asked us to come to Him as a little child." Mark 10:13-15

Open your heart to **the voices of the children** in this book and be open to the fact that God Himself longs for the fathers to turn their hearts toward their children in these last days and the disobedient to the wisdom of the righteous- **"to make ready a people prepared for Himself." Luke 1:17**

Daddy, if you only knew...

"I wish you would come home. I wish you never left. I feel bad. I wish to change you to a better person. I wish I could talk to you. I wish you would stop playing games."

8 Year Old Girl

Daddy, if you only knew...

"I miss you Daddy. If you only knew what I want you to do is know the Lord and I want you to come home. I will pray for you while you're in jail every night and day."

12 Year Old Boy

Daddy if you only knew...

"I miss you and I love you and I want you to get out of jail. And I want you to come home. And I want you to take me and my sisters somewhere."

Love,
7 Year Old Girl

Daddy, if you only knew...

"That I wanted to meet you and spend time with you. I want to know who you are. I want to live with you and spend my life with you. I want to know that you are there for me. I want to know that you want to spend time with me. Can you come one day and tell me about yourself? I want to know who you are and where you work at. I want to know your address and phone number. Do you have any other kids? Do I have any brothers and sisters and how old are they? Are they older than me? I want you to know that I met Jesus and that I like church. Do you know Jesus? Do you go to church? Do you want to come to my church? I would like to go to yours if you go. Your daughter."

12 Year Old Girl

II.

Let the Healing Begin

Steve Deal

Chapter 7

Dear Daddy, Dear Son & Daughter

Dear Daddy,
Dear Son & Daughter

By the time you read these words, my guess is that perhaps
you will have had your attention drawn to one or a number
of letters written by someone who could have been your son
or daughter. Possibly, you are flooded with emotion, regret, or
even anger at what has been written on these pages. These
authors are real sons and daughters who are writing to their
fathers. Some will never see their dad again.

For many, it is painful to write the reflections of a heart
that's been broken or a life that has been shattered by not
having the kind of relationship a father should have with
his children. Many of our society's ills are attributed directly
to fatherlessness. The enemy of your life would attempt to
destroy every home beginning with the head of the home, the
father. Satan's mission is to cause the male to be rendered
ineffective, emasculated, and to go AWOL (Absent Without
Leave). Men in our society have bought the lie that they don't
need to be in their children's lives, or they live in such a way
that it is in their children's best interest for them not to be
around. Or perhaps there have been circumstances, excuses,

situations (you can name them) that prohibit fathers from being there for their children.

It is possible you could be experiencing this reality presently. As you are reading the pages contained in this book, perhaps the remorse of not being the father you wish you could have been is plaguing you. Maybe you're experiencing the pain of rejection by your father and what is worse; you now are doing the same to your children. You might be reading this book simply because you have a desire to understand why those who are hurting around you have had to walk this path with their fathers.

Is there hope? You may ask. Perhaps you feel your situation is hopeless. How can you be a good father to your children? How can you forgive the father who rejected you, abused you, and lied to you? As long as you are on this side of the grave there is hope. Hope is desiring with expectation of good or a belief that it may be obtained; a desire of some good accompanied with at least a slight expectation of obtaining it, or a belief that is obtainable.

The compilation of letters put in this book is designed to give you hope after you work through the pain of your own failure as a father or of hurt inflicted upon you from your father. Not only do we want to impart hope to you, we want to bring healing to the damaged places in your soul, wholeness to the fragmented parts of your life, and restoration of relationships that have been lost.

If the truth were told, there is nothing I can say to help you fix your fatherhood problem. We can cry out to the "Father of the Fatherless" and His wisdom found only in His Word.

"Then they cried out to the Lord in their trouble, and He saved them from their distress. He sent forth His Word and healed them; He rescued them from the grave." Psalm 107:19, 20

It is our prayer that in the following pages you will discover, first and most importantly, who your Heavenly Father is; secondly, what a father should look like; and, thirdly, how you can be restored to be that kind of father. Again, as stated earlier, the answer to fatherhood (being a good daddy) lies in the pages of God's book, the Bible. You can expect to find the hope and encouragement you need in your life in the pages of His Word.

Chapter 8

A Wonderfully, Benevolent Father

A WONDERFULLY BENEVOLENT, FATHER

As our society is moving further and further away from
the moorings that made it great and kept it safe, a proper
understanding of the Heavenly Father has been lost. As a result,
many people's lives have been set adrift, wandering perilously into
the stormy seas of life with no safe haven. Fatherlessness is a by-
product of not having a relationship rooted in the foundation that
only Father God can give.

So how can you know your Heavenly Father? The first way to
know Him is to learn what He's not. Contrary to public opinion,
He is not waiting to judge and condemn you to Hell. In fact, the
opposite is true. He loves us and longs to have a relationship with
us, His creation. Remember, as mentioned earlier in this book, God
loves us one hundred percent all the time. Look at how Psalm 103
selected verses describes our Heavenly Father:

"THE LORD is compassionate and gracious, slow to anger,
abounding in love. He does not treat us as our sins deserve or
repay us according to our iniquities. For as high as the heavens
are above the earth, so great is His love for those who fear Him;
as far as the east is from the west, so far has He removed our

transgressions from us. As a father has compassion on his children, so the LORD has compassion on those who fear Him."

This doesn't sound like a father who's waiting to lower the boom on you if you miss-step in life. It does not sound like a father who is impatient and uncaring like many earthly fathers today. In fact, II Peter 3:9 says this about Him. "The Lord is not slow in keeping His promise, as some understand slowness. He is patient with you, not wanting anyone to perish, but everyone to come to repentance."

Permit me to reiterate the love He has for you and I, and all of His creation. Another look at His Love Letter to humanity will create an awareness of just how much He loves you. Why? Just because. Do you have to earn His love? Absolutely not! He loves you just because you are you! And you are the only one like you! You are the only one who has your DNA. When He made you, He broke the mold so to speak. Whether you love Him back or not that is your choice, but it doesn't change the fact that He loves you no matter what. The following words will revolutionize you in your understanding of your Heavenly Father.

"How great is the love the Father has lavished on us, that we should be called children of God! And that is what we are! The reason the world does not know us is that it did not know Him. Dear friends, now we are children of God, and what we will be has not yet been made known. But we know that when He appears, we shall be like Him, for we shall see Him as He is." I John 3:1, 2

His Love Letter further states that God is love. That means God equals love, and love equals God. Simple math. One is the same as the other, one love is embodied in the other. Your Heavenly Father takes love to the extreme by what He says in the following verse.

A Wonderfully Benevolent Father

"In this the love of God was manifested (made big, revealed, brought to light, understood in light of) toward us that God sent His one and only Son into the world (He voluntarily wrapped himself in human skin to walk this earth, sinless; the perfect one to die on our behalf in a spiritual sense) so that we could live through Him." 1 John 4:9 (NKJV)

Looking at the Heavenly Father from this perspective prayerfully (what his Book actually says about who He really is) will change your perspective. This is the first step to being a good father. The more I know Him and take my leading from Him, the better father I will become. Why? Because I was destined to be conformed into His image. I have only been delayed and distracted by sin, my own and the world's. It is not too late to change your perspective. As long as you are on this side of the grave, there is hope for you. How do you obtain this changed perspective, receiving this Loving Heavenly Father into your life? You need a spiritual heart transplant. Allow God, as the maker of new hearts, to remove your hard, unforgiving, angry, bitter, sinful heart and replace it with a soft, forgiving and pure one. This will give you a new lease on life.

The heart houses your spirit and is the seat that controls your mind, will, and emotions. How would your life be if it beat to the rhythm of the Father's Love? Just how do you get this new heart? By surrendering it to the operation of the Great Physician, Jesus. Let Him replace your dark, dead heart with the light of His love, and He will make your heart alive again. How do you get to know your Heavenly Father? Ask Him. Pray this prayer or just express your forgiveness to Him as you would long and desire to speak to your father.

Prayer to Know Your Heavenly Father

"Father in Heaven, I want to know You. The only way I can know You is through the way You have provided Your Son, Jesus. I invite His person into my life. Jesus, I recognize that I have made a mess of my life and that my life has been marked by failure. You call this condition sin, and I know You died on the cross so I do not have to die spiritually. Please forgive me of what You call sin and what I know to be sin and replace my sinful heart with a new one. I commit to turn my life from my old sinful life and turn towards you. As a result of this prayer, I know I now have a Heavenly Father who loves me and calls me His child."

Chapter 9

Here's Looking at You, Dad!

Chapter 9

HERE'S LOOKING AT YOU, DAD!

Many men, particularly in the United States, which is primarily my frame of reference, have not had good models as fathers. I was one of them growing up. My own father was addicted to alcohol for as long as I can remember. Needless to say, his parenting skills were severely affected by his lifestyle choice. Notice I called it a lifestyle choice instead of a disease. Calling it a disease takes away the responsibility each of us has to rectify what is not right in our lives.

Once we come to grips with what is wrong with our perspective, our thought processing, and ultimately our behavior as a result of how we have chosen to live, then the healing can begin. This is something my father never did, and as a result, he died an alcoholic's death, family-less, friendless, and penniless. Because of the alcoholism, he wasn't able to be a good father to my brothers and I. This affected us at various levels, some of which we are still dealing with to this day.

I might be inclined to tell you all the changes and heartache my father put us through, but it won't serve any redeeming purposes other than giving you a perspective of my identification with your situation. I will tell you that despite what I experienced, I made a determination to do three things in my life that helped me become the father that I am today.

The first decision I made out of the gates into my adulthood was not to be the kind of father he was. Even to the extent that when I presided over his funeral, I was able to sincerely thank him for giving me an example that I didn't want to follow. He left a legacy, if you will, of something I didn't want to ever be like. His character that was produced by his lifestyle motivated me to want to be the exact opposite. In this case, a man who by God's grace has at the top of his list the desire to be a godly father. It is right up there with being a faithful servant of Christ Jesus my Lord and a faithful husband to my wife. In fact, my ultimate goals are relatively straightforward and simple and they are as follows:

Love and Serve God and His People

Decision number one was to love and serve God and His people, first and foremost my wife and then my children. Then to be an agent of change to the world with whom I come in contact on behalf of God. I figure with these priorities in line, everything else will be taken care of. Jesus tells us "But seek first His Kingdom and His righteousness, and all these things will be given to you as well." Matthew 6:33

This decision not to be the kind of father my Dad was, helped me to prioritize what is most important in our lives as a whole. One response I had to my own Dad's lack of involvement in my life was to never miss a game, a dance recital, a concert, a graduation, an award ceremony or any other thing that my children deemed important. I was and am blessed to have been able to take them to school and pick them up. I enjoy hanging around with my own kids and my "spiritual" children that have practically lived in my home from time to time. I just like being there, even if I don't say anything. Kids are not always inclined to talk to their parents, no matter how close you are, particularly during the teenage years, but I am there if the mood strikes them.

Forgive My Father Wholly "Holy"

The next decision I made was to forgive my father. While I acknowledge that my father's behavior towards my brothers and me was unacceptable, I had to walk in forgiveness towards him. This wasn't difficult because I was able to differentiate between his behavior and my worth as a person. I was somehow able to realize as a young person that his physical and verbal abuse towards me was not my fault. It was connected to his disease, (not alcoholism, but the disease of sin) yet I still needed to forgive.

"For if you forgive men when they sin against you, your Heavenly Father will also forgive you, but if you do not forgive men their sins, your Heavenly Father will not forgive your sins." Matthew 6:14-15

Chapter 10

Break the Lies of Rejection

Chapter 10

BREAK THE LIES OF REJECTION

The last decision I made was not to own the lies that come with the rejection or perceived rejection from my father. I recognized that something was not right, and there were lies of which the enemy would try to convince me. Lies that my father didn't love me, and that his inability to be there for me due to his alcoholism was a sign of rejection.

Whenever I was wrestling with rejection, I reminded myself that everything that I am is attributed to God's grace alone. Secondly, I am the work of His hands in Christ Jesus to do good works. Lastly, He (God the Father) chose me before the foundation of the world that I should be holy (perfect) and without blame before Him in love, having predestined us to adoption as sons by Jesus Christ, Himself. He made us accepted as His sons (Ephesians 1). I also am his favorite and you are too!

Because of these three goals, I have been able to develop and maintain a healthy relationship with my own kids as well as other spiritual kids I have helped to raise across this nation. I say, "maintain" because that word means "to keep in good condition or in working order by checking or repairing it regularly!" The job is never done.

Our problem as naturally flawed humans is and always has been a faulty perspective, which was skewed at the fall. This is where the image of God, in which we were made, was marred by sin. Because of this, humanity developed an image problem, resulting in us not fulfilling our God-given responsibility of maintaining dominion ("dominion" meaning sovereignty; or control) on the earth.

"Then God said, 'Let Us make man in Our image, according to Our likeness and let them rule over all the earth.' So God created man in His own image; in the image of God He created them." Genesis 1:26, 27

As a result we're not able in our own ability to comprehend our intended responsibility, which was given to us at creation. This affects our relationships from the head down. This means that if our relationship with our Creator, Father God, is messed up, then consequently our ability to relate to women and children is messed up. Our hope is that a message can come forth from our mess.

The God-man Jesus, who by His death gave us the opportunity for a completely different and redeemed perspective, makes what seemed impossible, due to our flawed human perspective, possible. A changed perspective of our understanding of Father God will help us to be the fathers we hope to be. Why? Because it is His love for us that took away the veil between the Father's heart and His creation, the ones He calls sons and daughters.

"For He Himself is our peace, who has made the two one, and has the barrier, the dividing wall of hostility...For through Him we both have access to the Father by one Spirit." Ephesians 2:14 & 18

But God demonstrates his own love for us in this: While we were still sinners (having our perspective obscured by sin) Christ died for us." Romans 5:8

Chapter 11

I Can Be a Godly Father?

I CAN BE A GODLY FATHER?

It is our prayer as we ink the last pages of this book that the hope of being a godly father can be restored and perhaps even more than hope, the actual commitment to a life that reflects the Father heart of God. From our perspective, we have found that fatherhood is best epitomized in the pages of God's eternal Word to humanity.

Perhaps, there are books and articles written about being good dads. We are also aware of the efforts by organizations and ministries that emphasize the importance of proper fatherhood. While these have their place, and have had varying degrees of effectiveness, our approach here has been to capture the child's heart as it relates to their fathers. Every one of us is a child of a father, yet not all of us have had the kind of relationship we desired or needed with our own fathers. For those reading this of male persuasion perhaps there is a longing to be the father your children can look up to, relate to, and respect.

It is from this approach we look once again to the Words of the perfectly loving Father God. It is Him we turn to find the hope of being a good father. You may ask yourself the question, "Can I be a godly father?" It may seem impossible based on your personal history. The great news is that the Father is always present, all seeing, all knowing, and all powerful. He is also a forgiving Father, extending His benevolence to us as naturally flawed humans.

We conclude then that being a godly father is entirely possible because He did what we possibly could not do in that He died to bring us hope of a changed perspective and now we can see how to love as the Father loved us. Eugene Peterson describes the magnitude of the Father's love for us, His children in "The Message" Bible:

"What marvelous love the Father has extended to us! Just look at it – we're called children of God! That's who we really are. But that's also why the world doesn't recognize us or take us seriously, because it has no idea who He is or what He's been up to. Friends, that's exactly who we are: children of God. And that's only the beginning...this is how we come to understand and experience love: Christ sacrificed His life for us. This is why we ought to live sacrificially for our fellow believers, our wives, our children, and not just be out for ourselves." I John 3, paraphrased

If you and I understand our position as children of the Father God, and that He now dwells by His Spirit in each of us, we can model the love of the Father to our own children.

We must realize as men that it's not just about us, and that the world does not revolve around us. As we begin to lay down our personal agendas and selfish desires, we will see this world that we live in begin to turn completely around for the good. It is time to heed the voice of Father God as we truly "hear the voices of the children."

Chapter 12

From Generation to Generation

FROM GENERATION
TO GENERATION

(These are letters from Lennette's father to his dad, Lennette to her father, Steve to his dad, and both of Steve and Lennette's children to their dad, Steve.)

Dad was born March 15, 1893 and went home to Glory on May 5, 1990. He was 97 years old, and he wanted to make a 100 or the rapture, whichever came first. He so reverenced his parents by calling them Ma and Pa with such affection. Grandpa Cheek, whom I never saw, took Dad out of school when he was in the second lesson of the second reader, and put him to work in the coal mines of West Virginia in 1903. This was during the big strike Dad so often referred to as the "hard life days". Dad never went back to school. He would write to me at times on whatever was available, the back of a calendar, or a paid off note at the bank. Dad always used the small *i's* so I kept most of his notes. Having a good work ethic, Dad seemed to always have a job of some sort, though we never lived, as he would say "high on the hog." We got by with the necessities of life and old cars. We never took a vacation, but Dad loved to hunt, and he took some time off for a hunting trip each year.

Some time in the late 40s, Dad was saved under the ministry of Reverend Bob Doan, and was one of the finest Christians

Daddy, If You Only Knew

I have ever known. In 1951, I was on leave from the Marines at Christmas time. At this time Bob Doan was preaching at our home Freewill Baptist Church, and Dad invited me to the altar to pray with me for salvation. Rev. Doan drove from Orlando, Florida to West Virginia at the age of 83, to preach Dad's funeral. This was a great honor to us.

Dad, because of our family's hardships, and his love of the Lord, had such a Christian heart. I have seen him pick up fallen apples by the side of the road, and drive several miles to deliver them to someone in need. Though we lived in West Virginia, I saw Dad take three bags of food to Virginia and give them to people he saw in need on his last visit. I was with him once on Christmas morning while he was on leave. He drove to an open store just to purchase a complete Christmas dinner for a neighbor in need. Only then did he say, "Lets go home, I can eat now that I know they have dinner." He was a soul winner, seeing at least eight of his former drinking and hunting buddies saved before he died.

Dad was the nation's number one husband to the girl he was married to for 64 ½ years. After all that time, Mom was still his sweetheart, and strangely enough, he died 64 ½ days after Mom died. I could write a book about Dad, so I will have to stop here. In 1983, I taped Dad for three hours on his life and our family. What a treasured possession to listen to from time to time. Though I listen to his voice, I know exactly where he, oops, they are.

Sincerely, Arthur M. Cheek

Dear Daddy,

"If you only knew that every time I saw you hold mom's hand wherever you went, I was watching. It made me want to marry a man who would hold my hand wherever we went.

Daddy, did you know that I loved the way you openly kissed mom even when my friends were around. I can distinctly remember one of my friends going into the kitchen to get something and they abruptly returned with their hands empty. When I asked why, they said that they caught you and mom kissing. I replied, "Oh, that's normal," go back and get what you need." I loved that being normal. I wanted to marry a man who would openly kiss me in front of our kids and their friends and it be considered normal. It made me feel secure knowing that you loved mom that openly. Of course I figured you must love her that much privately. I hoped it stopped at a kiss because it was "gross" to think of your parents in any other way (Ha-ha). Did you know that I loved it when you told me how beautiful my mom was? I wanted to marry a guy who told me how beautiful I was.

Did you know that I noticed how you stayed up most nights, late, grading papers for your students and making phone calls to parents, not just to express concern, but to say, "Your son (daughter) did

great today." I heard those words. I also saw your
disappointment when you hung up the phone from
parents who did not care, because you cared. How
lucky I thought those children were to have you as
their teacher. It was evident your students loved you
because you got more presents at Christmas from
your students than we got you. It still strikes me
funny at how cluttered your home office remains,
because you refuse to get rid of some of the student's
gifts, even though you retired over 25 years ago.

Did you know that I will never forget the
compassion you showed me when my knee went
through the kitchen wall leaving a huge hole? I
just knew I was dead because I shouldn't have been
"hosing my sister" down with the new nozzle on the
kitchen sink. I just couldn't help myself. Who would
have thought I would go sliding across the kitchen
floor trying to escape Christie's revenge. You were
more concerned for my well-being because you saw I
was in pain than you were the huge hole in the wall.
Thanks Dad.

Did you know that I will never forget your response
to me when I locked my keys in the car at school for
the 12th time my senior year. I was so embarrassed
to call you at work and get you out of class to tell
you I locked my keys in the car again. So I decided
to enlist the help of friends to break in. Do you
remember that day? My friend ended up smashing

my car window into a thousand pieces. I so wish I had humbled myself and called you earlier. Now I had to tell you I locked my keys in the car for the 12th time AND I broke the car window. Instead of yelling at me (which I was expecting and deserved) you told me where you had some extra money saved at home so I could get the window fixed right away. You kindly reminded me to call the next time I locked my keys in the car before trying to "break in." Thanks Dad.

Did you know that I will forever be grateful that although you were a teacher, you never required more of Christie and I than OUR best? You never compared us. Thanks Dad.

Did you know that I love your jokes even though I don't usually get them (ha-ha) because it shows me you can always find time to help someone laugh? How do you memorize all those jokes?

Did you know that I love the fact that you always tell mom, Christie, and I that you love us and how thankful I am that you have extended that amazing gift to my own kids and husband? Did you know that I am so thankful that you and mom have been happily married for 50 years? Did you know that I will never take for granted the fact that you pray for me and many others every night for an hour before you go to bed? Did you know that I am so thankful that you didn't just talk Jesus, but you lived like Jesus? Did you know I feel like the most blessed girl (woman) in the world because I have a godly daddy like you? For all of these reasons I dedicate this book to you (and mom)!

I Love you Daddy, Lennette Deal

From Generation to Generation

Daddy, if you only knew...

The impact you would have on my life, only not in the way one might expect. This may sound a little weird, but thanks for being an example that I didn't want to emulate. Everything that you were not as a father, I have become.

I thank you that by watching your life, I did not allow myself to become addicted to alcohol like you did. I also thank you that your decision to not be there for me caused me to make sure I was there for my kids.

You never took me to school. You never watched my football, basketball, and baseball games. Nor were you there for other significant times in my life. The Lord has graced me to be in a position to attend every one of my children's games. Sometimes I have coached their games or been a "dance" parent. I still drive my kids and their friends to where they need to go. I love being a taxi-dad.

Though you were unfaithful to mom, I have been faithful to my children's mother and my wife.

Most importantly, though Christ Jesus was not Lord of your life, He became the center point from which my whole world emanates. I love God and serve Him, and yes, though you did not go to church with us, my family and I go all the time. It's not out of some sort of religious duty or obligation. It's because we want to.

You did go to church a couple of times when I was well into my calling as a Pastor. Both times you came, I was preaching at a large church. I know it must have been overwhelming for you, seeing me, your eldest son, in front of all those people telling them what God could do for them from His Word. Both times you came to the altar crying. I am not sure if they were tears of repentance, or that you were proud of me, or if it was regret mixed with the tears that reeked of alcohol and cigarettes. Nevertheless, you came and hugged me. You told me how proud you were of me and then I led you in the sinner's prayer.

A few years later as you were on your deathbed with cirrhosis of the liver as a result of decades of alcohol abuse, you once again prayed with me to make sure your life was right with the Lord. Believing that confession to have been sincere in your heart, we know that when you passed from this life to the next, that you found yourself immediately in the presence of the Lord.

Days later, you were pronounced dead at the same hospital where we had prayed earlier. I made your funeral arrangements. Unfortunately not many came, not your mother, sister, brother, friends, or other extended family. It was just your three sons, your ex-wife (my mother), your girlfriend of many years, and your grandchildren (Jordan and Brianna). my wife and her parents also attended, as well as my wife's sister with her daughter.

I don't recall crying, only feeling a sense of sadness. You had so much potential! You were the best looking guy in your high school class; intelligent and athletic. You could have been a doctor, but your life was wasted. Yet out of sadness there sprung up hope. Hope for the next generation that I would be the kind of father I wish I had growing up. For that I thank you because what you did not do became great motivation for me to be a father to many. If that's the legacy you left, I am thankful to be a part of it. That's the beauty of the right-side up, upside-down Kingdom. What may have begun wrong or what potentially could have gone wrong, the power and grace of God can make it right. So thanks, Dad, for helping me to connect to my real Father. He calls the shots in my life. It makes sense because my Daddy is the God of the Universe, yet He stoops down to become intimately acquainted with each of us.

The problems I had growing up have now become the process by which providence worked in my life. All is forgiven, Dad, and turned into thanks. I am who I am because of your life and the direction it caused me to run to and away from.

Thanks and Love from Your Son,

Steve Deal

Daddy, if you only knew...

"I love and appreciate you more than you will ever know. You have been, and continue to be, the best father anyone could ever have.

I admire you so much. You are the greatest Father in the world! You rose above everything that said you couldn't be a good father and chose to be the best. You are the most amazing man of God I have ever known and will ever know. No matter who I meet, that fact will remain the same. The life you have lived in secret and at home with us is the greatest testimony there is. I love you, your son.

Jordan Deal to his father Steve Deal
21 years old

Daddy, if you only knew…

"You are the best daddy I could ever have. I am so thankful for you. You are a gift from God. I am sorry about your daddy. I know he drank and got drunk, but when someone called you to come get him, you were there in a flash. Even if you found him in his house on the couch drunk or if you found him in the dumpster, being a bum in the street because he was so drunk. But I admire you because you gave him respect as a man of God. I am glad that when he was in the hospital you helped him give his heart to the Lord. Hopefully he is in heaven now with my Heavenly Daddy.

Dad, even though we've also had some ups and downs I still love you. I am proud that you are my father and Jesus is my Heavenly Father. I love you daddy and I know that you love me too. Thank you for being a man of God. Thank you for being my pastor and my daddy. Thank you Jesus for being my Heavenly Father. Dad, really, I love you."

Brianna Deal to her father Steve Deal
At the time of this writing she was 13 years old.

III.
Hope
In Action

"Children, obey your parents in the Lord, for this is right. 'Honor your father and mother' which is the first commandment with a promise 'that it may go well with you and that you may enjoy long life on the earth.' "
Ephesians 6:1-3

YOUR HOPE IN ACTION

It is NOT too late to start honoring your mother and father, even if it can only be words of respect that flow from your lips because they are no longer there. We encourage you to write to your daddy and begin your healing.** Just begin by saying "Daddy, if you only knew..."

**5 Fold Media does not encourage writing disturbing, disrespectful, or negative content to your parents.

WHAT'S NEXT?

There is a sequel to this book that will be released as soon as all of the letters have been collected. The title of the sequel is **"If I Had Only Known."** This book will house the voices of the fathers who would have lived life differently "if they had only known" the impact their choices would have had on their children, as well as those fathers who want to reflect on how thankful they are for their good choices. There are great dads who have been there for their children, who have made their children a priority, and who have evaluated every decision they have made based on their well-being. We want this book to house these letters as well. We can all learn something from the men who choose to participate in this book.

If you are interested in being a part of this book, go to our website at www.realdealministries.com for instructions. We ask that you write the letter in Word format and then submit it as an attachment. We won't be able to use every letter, but we will prayerfully consider each one submitted. If your letter is selected for the publication of the book, **"If I Had Only Known,"** your name will not be used to protect your identity and the identity of your children. Therefore, do not use the names of your children in your letter or other individuals who might wish to be unidentified.

Thank you,
Steve and Lennette Deal

ABOUT THE AUTHORS

Steve and Lennette Deal are highly motivated speakers with an authority on placing a God-given honor back upon the family.

To contact Steve & Lennette visit:
www.realdealministries.com

5 Fold Media, LLC is a Spirit-led, for-profit media company. Our desire is to produce lasting fruit in writing, music, art, and creative gifts.

Get your book published!

For more information visit:
www.5foldmedia.com

APOSTLES
PROPHETS
EVANGELISTS
PASTORS
TEACHERS

LaVergne, TN USA
11 June 2010
185794LV00005B/1/P